Birthdays

Birthdays

LIFE, LIBERTY, AND THE PURSUIT OF CAKE

EDITED BY ELLEN CARNAHAN

ILLUSTRATED BY DUFF ORLEMANN

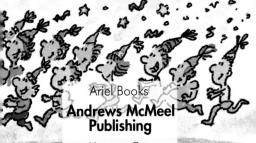

Ariel Books

Andrews McMeel Publishing

Kansas City

ISBN: 0-8362-3599-1

Library of Congress Catalog Card Number: 97-71524

Contents

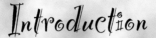

Introduction

A birthday can mean different things to different people. To some it's a day for private reflection and quiet celebration with close friends and family. Others may spend it on a shopping spree or an ice-cream binge. Still others take their birthday as an excuse to go

$\mathscr{B}irthdays$

wild, dance all night, and wake up the next morning wearing a lamp-shade or someone else's shirt.

Some people like a great big party, others want lots of presents, and the truly serene are content if the sun merely comes up and stays up! Whatever your preference, you're *supposed* to let yourself be enter-tained on your birthday, or at least treat yourself well. After all, the rest of the year you've been either working hard or working harder. You deserve some recognition for having made it this far in life!

So, pour yourself a birthday beverage, put your feet up, and celebrate your special day with this collection of birthday wit and wisdom—quotations from the young and the old, the silly and the serious, the musing and the mirthful.

Happy Birthday!

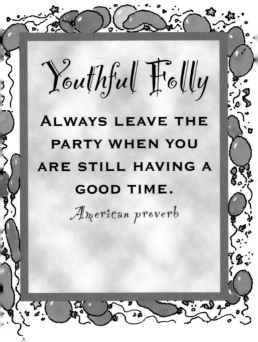

Youthful Folly

ALWAYS LEAVE THE PARTY WHEN YOU ARE STILL HAVING A GOOD TIME.

American proverb

Birthdays

I believe that one has to be seventy before one is full of courage. The young are always halfhearted.

—D. H. LAWRENCE

Birthdays

At sixteen I was stupid,
confused, insecure, and
indecisive. At twenty-five I
was wise, self-confident,
prepossessing, and as-

AGE 16

14

AGE 25

Youthful Folly

sertive. At forty-five, I am stupid, confused, insecure, and indecisive. Who would have supposed that maturity is only a short break in adolescence?

—JULES FEIFFER

AGE 45

15

Birthdays

He who laughs, lasts.

—LEO ROSTEN

Youthful Folly

Young, a donkey;
old, an ass.

—YIDDISH PROVERB

Birthdays

Age is nothing but a num-
ber. It is how you
use it.

—ETHEL PAYNE

18

. Everything that's fun is
either illegal, immoral,
or fattening.

—AMERICAN PROVERB

Birthdays

Fifty years old, 212 fights, and I'm still pretty.

—MUHAMMAD ALI

Birthdays

The secret of staying young is to live honestly, eat slowly, and lie about your age.

—LUCILLE BALL

24

Birthdays

If you want to stay young, associate with youth. If you want to get old quickly, try to keep up with them.

—ANONYMOUS

Birthdays

The true test of maturity is not how old a person is but how he reacts to awakening in the midtown area in his shorts.

—WOODY ALLEN

The youth gets together his materials to build a bridge to the moon . . . and, at length, the middle-aged man concludes to build a woodshed with them.

—HENRY DAVID THOREAU

Birthdays

A woman past forty should make up her mind to be young, not her face.

—BILLIE BURKE

Respect Your Elders

**LET US RESPECT
GRAY HAIRS,
ESPECIALLY OUR
OWN.**

J. P. Senn

Birthdays

When I was a boy of fourteen, my father was so ignorant I could hardly stand to have the old man around. But when I got to be twenty-one, I was astonished at how much the old man had learned in seven years.

—MARK TWAIN

Birthdays

An archaeologist is the best husband any woman can have; the older she gets, the more interested he is in her.

—AGATHA CHRISTIE

38

Birthdays

Years ago we discovered
the exact point, the dead
center of middle age. It
occurs when you are too
young to take up golf
and too old to rush up to
the net.

—FRANKLIN P. ADAMS

40

Respect Your Elders

My grandmother started walking five miles a day when she was sixty. She's ninety-seven now, and we don't know where the hell she is.

—ELLEN DeGENERES

Birthdays

What he hath scanted men in hair, he hath given them in wit.

—WILLIAM SHAKESPEARE

No spring, nor summer
    beauty hath such grace,
As I have seen in one
    autumnal face.

—JOHN DONNE

SPRING   SUMMER   AUTUMN

I'm at an age when my back goes out more than I do.

—PHYLLIS DILLER

Birthdays

I'm at the age where food has taken the place of sex in my life. In fact, I've just had a mirror put over my kitchen table.

—RODNEY DANGERFIELD

Birthdays

Old age is like a plane flying through a storm. Once you're aboard, there's nothing you can do. You can't stop the plane; you can't stop the storm; you can't stop time. So one might as well accept it calmly, wisely.

—GOLDA MEIR

Birthdays

Sometimes, when I realize I
am 101 years old, it hits
me right between the eyes.
I say, "Oh Lord, how did
this happen?" Turning one
hundred was the worst
birthday of my life. I
wouldn't wish it on my
worst enemy. Turning 101

Respect Your Elders

was not so bad. Once
you're past that century
mark, it's just not as
shocking.

—BESSIE DELANY

Respect Your Elders

The age of a woman
doesn't mean a thing.
The best tunes are played
on the oldest fiddles.

—SIGMUND Z. ENGEL

Birthdays

A man of forty today has
nothing to worry him but
falling hair, inability to
button the top button, fail-
ing vision, shortness of
breath, a tendency of the
collar to shut off all
breathing, trembling of the

kidneys to whatever tune
the orchestra is playing,
and a general
sense of giddi-
ness when the
matter of rent
is brought up.

—ROBERT BENCHLEY

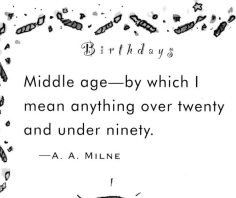

ℬirthdays

Middle age—by which I mean anything over twenty and under ninety.

—A. A. MILNE

"Don't worry about senil-
ity," my grandfather used
to say. "When it hits you,
you won't know it."

—BILL COSBY

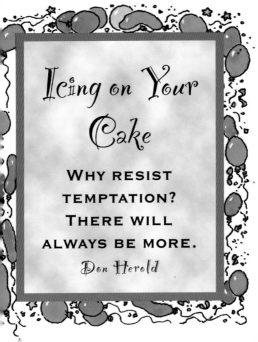

Icing on Your Cake

WHY RESIST TEMPTATION? THERE WILL ALWAYS BE MORE.

Don Herold

FOUNTAIN OF YOUTH

You're never too old to get younger.

—MAE WEST

I'll keep going till my face falls off.

—BARBARA CARTLAND

Icing on Your Cake

I'll be around as long
as the horses think I'm
smarter than they are.

—JAMES E. "SUNNY JIM"

FITZSIMMONS

A man's only as old as
the woman he feels.

—GROUCHO MARX

Birthdays

Who says I am old?
Is an old man like this?
Heart welcomes sweet
   flowers,
Laughter floats over fra-
   grant cups:

Icing on Your Cake

What can I do, what can I
say?
My hoary hair floats in the
spring wind.

—KIM CHONG-GU

Birthdays

Age gives good advice
when it is no longer able
to give a bad example.

—AMERICAN PROVERB

Icing on Your Cake

The great pleasure in
life is doing what people
say you cannot do.

—WALTER BAGEHOT

When somebody says to me—which they do like every five years—"How does it feel to be over the hill?" my response is, "I'm just heading up the mountain."

—JOAN BAEZ

Birthdays

May all your future years
be
Free from disappointment,
care or strife,
That every birthday you
will be
A little more in love with
life.

—ANONYMOUS

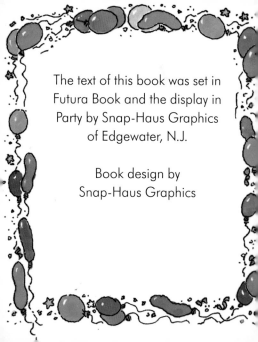

The text of this book was set in
Futura Book and the display in
Party by Snap-Haus Graphics
of Edgewater, N.J.

Book design by
Snap-Haus Graphics